How to Clean Toilets

And other things your Mom should have taught you about cleaning Bathrooms

By

Rachel Redden

Health Learning Series

Mendon Cottage Books

JD-Biz Publishing

Table of Contents

Introduction 3
Deep Cleaning 4
Cabinet 5
Dusting 6
The Mirror 7
Soap Dish 9
Sink 11
Tubs/Showers 13
Shower Curtain 15
Bidets 17
Commode (toilet) 18
Rugs 20
Toilet Brush and Cup 22
Floors 24
Garbage's 26
Time 27
Monthly Routine 28
Weekly Routine 29
Daily Routine 30
Types of Bathroom Ware 31
Apparel 33
Cleaning supplies 35
Cleaning on a budget 37
Tips 38
Conclusion 40
Author Bio 41
Publisher 50

Introduction

The bathroom has to be the most used room in the entire house, but nobody wants to clean it. Why? Well for starters, it's a disgusting job, but I think you'll agree that cleaning a bathroom is a task that is not to be taken too lightly, it can cause sickness or worse if you just let it be. It's a big job most of the time and often we don't know where to start, a lot of the time and we tend to leave it until it is so filthy that we can no longer stand it. But I think we can all agree that there is nothing more disgusting than going to someone's house and using a filthy bathroom. I once went to a friend's house and had to use their bathroom. The stench in that room nearly killed me off! So I decided I would rather go in my pants than use that bathroom (I didn't if you wanted to know. We left for home before I went to those drastic measures). So even if it's just for the neighbors we should clean it. Though it doesn't excuse the fact that it is a big job every single time you clean it. Well, I'm here to tell you that even deep cleaning it can be less of a big deal when you know how to go about it. All it takes is a plan, some rags, cleaners and some desire.

Deep Cleaning

I'll start off with the deep cleaning procedure first, then move down to the monthly, then weekly and then daily.

Start with putting your cleaners into the sink, tub/shower, commode and bidet.
1. Wet the sides of the sink, tub/shower, commode and bidet.
2. Pour your cleaners round the sides, and let them soak.
3. Move everything that can be moved out.

Cabinet

When deep cleaning, helps to get rid of the clutter in your cabinet and for some it is refreshing to reorganize it.

1. Start with taking everything out.
2. Wipe out the shelves and drawers.
3. Organize the contents of your cabinet in any way you like, let others who are living with you know where everything is in case they need anything.
4. Get rid of anything that doesn't need to be in there, either put it where it belongs, give to the person it belongs to, claim it, or throw it away.
5. Dust and clean anything that goes back in the cabinet.
6. Put it all back.

Dusting

This, besides getting the dusting out of the way, will keep you from cleaning the floor or other surfaces over again because the dust bunnies often are obvious when they land on the already vacuumed floor or wiped of sinks and such.

1. Get a damp rag and if you desire, a dry rag to dry everything after you've wiped up all the dust.
2. Go from top: Pictures, on top of the bathroom cabinet, the mirror and anything else you might have on the walls.
3. To bottom: The cabinet doors, drawers, base boards, and the bottom of the sink.
4. Hairs are a bit tricky, just grab a paper towel, get it damp but usable, wipe up wherever you see the hairs and throw it away.

The Mirror

The mirror does not require any specific tactic or cleaner; all you need are two rags; a wet one and a dry one.

1. Adjust the mirror if it needs adjusting. Also if it is surrounded by lights and hung on the wall rather than attached it might be a good idea to adjust it and let all the dead bugs fall out.
2. If bugs fall out just sweep them off the sink or counter and continue cleaning.
3. Take the wet rag and wipe down the mirror until all the toothpaste and water specks disappear.

4. Take the dry rag and wipe down the mirror until the streaks are gone.

Soap Dish

The soap dish you wouldn't think would need to be cleaned all that often but it is one of the things you'll definitely want to shine for your own sanity as well as when you have company.

1. Take out the bar of soap and set it aside. The wet side up if you don't want additional mess.
2. Turn on the faucet and run it under the water for a minute.
3. Scrub it out until all the dried soap comes off.
4. Dry and polish it, put the soap back in and set it aside until you get the sink done.

5. If you don't deal with bar soap very much but prefer to use liquid hand soap, it is just as important to make sure that is clean as well.
6. Pull off the soap build-up around the tip where the soap comes out.
7. Just get your rag around it and wash it lightly until you can't feel the soap at all.

Sink

The sink besides the mirror and the soap dish is probably the easiest to clean. You'll have had the cleaner soaking in the sink so it won't be too hard to scrub the grime off of everything.

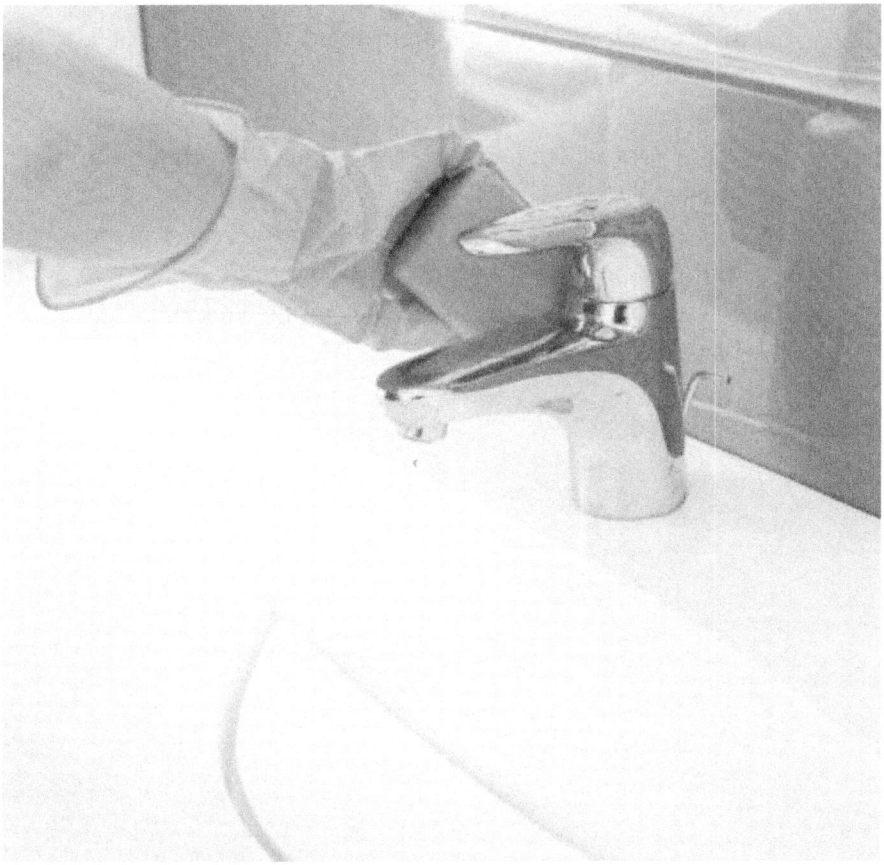

1. Keep your wet and dry rag from the mirror and use them for the rest of the bathroom.
2. Start at the faucet and fixtures and scrub them till you're sure you've cleaned them.
3. Scrub at the back and around the faucet and fixtures and move around till you've scrubbed all the sides.

4. If your sink is not set in a counter, then you'll want to wash around the outside of the sink because water sometimes gets on the outsides and leaves water marks.
5. If it is, remove everything on the counter and wash it until you can't see any water marks.
6. Scrub the inside of the sink until you can slide your rag across the surface and have it ride as smooth as glass.
7. Rinse your rag until the majority of the soap is gone then rinse the rest of your sink starting at the faucet and fixtures.
8. Take your dry rag and dry and polish everything until it shines.
9. Wash what you took off the counter if it needs it and dry it before you put it back on.
10. Put everything that usually goes on the sink or counter back on.

Tubs/Showers

Tubs are pretty much just a bigger version of the sink. The reason they are harder is because, well, they're bigger and they have the hard to reach tile wall behind them. Showers are pretty much the same way except there is much more wall space.

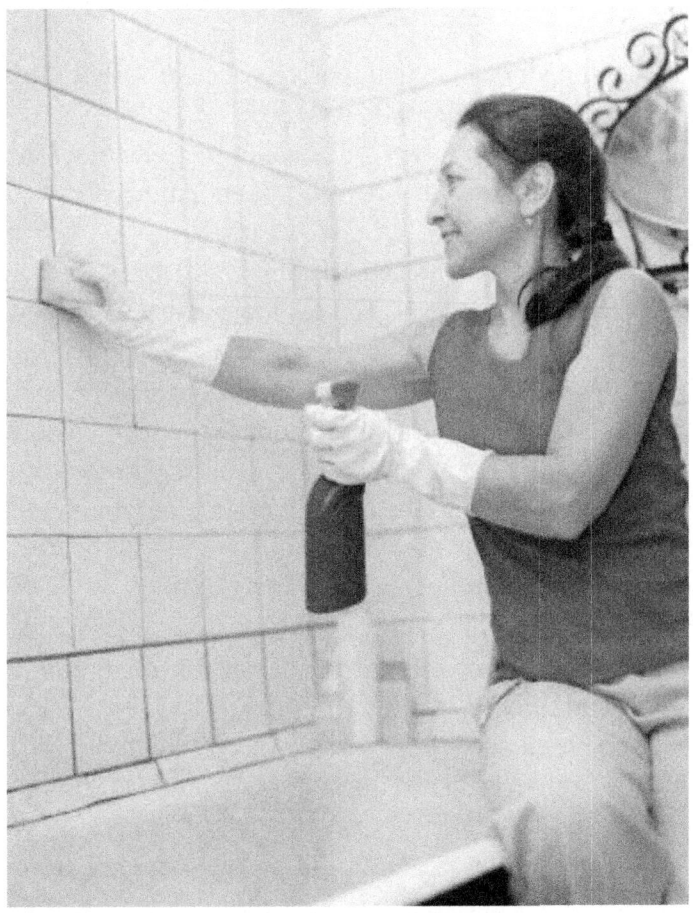

1. Take out the soaps and razors and scrubs and such.
2. Get a spray bottle filled with vinegar and water and spray down everything in the tub/shower.

3. Start with the back wall first. This way you can just stand in the tub or shower space and reduce the chances of ruining your back by leaning way over.
4. Scrub the shower head, faucet and fixtures. If the shower head comes off of the wall and is covered with hard water, then get a bucket of vinegar and water and stick it in. leave it until everything comes off easily. You might have to wipe it off a few times if the hard water is really caked on there.
5. Let the vinegar soak in before you start scrubbing, it will make everything really easy.
6. Break the wall down into smaller sections like four square tiles or eight, so that it won't be so tedious and aggravating.
7. Rinse and dry walls and fixtures.
8. If the grout between the tiles looks a little dark and frankly, disgusting; here's a recipe I found on *Practically Functional* that really helps: get ¾ cup baking soda, and ¼ cup Clorox. Mix it together to make a thick past. Stick the paste on the grout lines and let it sit for five to ten minutes.
9. Afterwards scrub the paste into the grout lines again and wait another five to ten minutes.
10. After that, rinse the paste off and let it dry.
11. Scrub around the sides of the tub.
12. Then move down to the insides of the tub. Scrub till they feel as smooth as glass.
13. The bottom will be about the same, though the surface will be a little rougher to don't be discouraged if it doesn't feel very smooth.
14. Rinse out your rag and rinse off the sides and insides of the tub dry and polish to your desire.

Shower Curtain

The shower curtain probably has to be the most difficult if you don't know how to do it.

1. Check the label and see if it is machine washable.
2. If it's not, you might want to get one so you don't have to have a wrestling match every time you want to clean it.
3. If it is, take it off the pole and take off the hooks.
4. Add a little ammonia to your detergent.
5. Throw it in the wash on a warm gentle cycle.

6. If you're unsure about how your dryer will treat it then hang it up to dry over the stairway banister or just hand it back up again.
7. If it isn't, then follow the directions on the care tag.
8. Now if you have sliding glass doors, you can treat it just as you would a window or the other walls if hard water has settled there.
9. Now the shower door tracks are a little harder. Squirt an all-purpose cleaner in and around the tracks and let it sit to help dissolve anything hard that could be in there.
10. Now get a screw driver and wrap a rag around it.
11. Stick it in where you can and wipe it out.

Bidets

Not many Americans know about bidets, as they are mostly in Europe. They are kind of a small bath that you sit in. It looks kind of like a commode.

1. Bidets can be cleaned in the same way as sinks and tubs.
2. Wash the faucet and fixtures.
3. Wash around the sides and the undersides.
4. Then wash in the bowl of it.
5. Rinse your rag and then rinse the bidet.
6. Then dry it.

Commode (toilet)

Commodes pretty much have the same technique as the sinks, tubs and generally the whole bathroom. Start in the place with the least germs and make your way to the most.

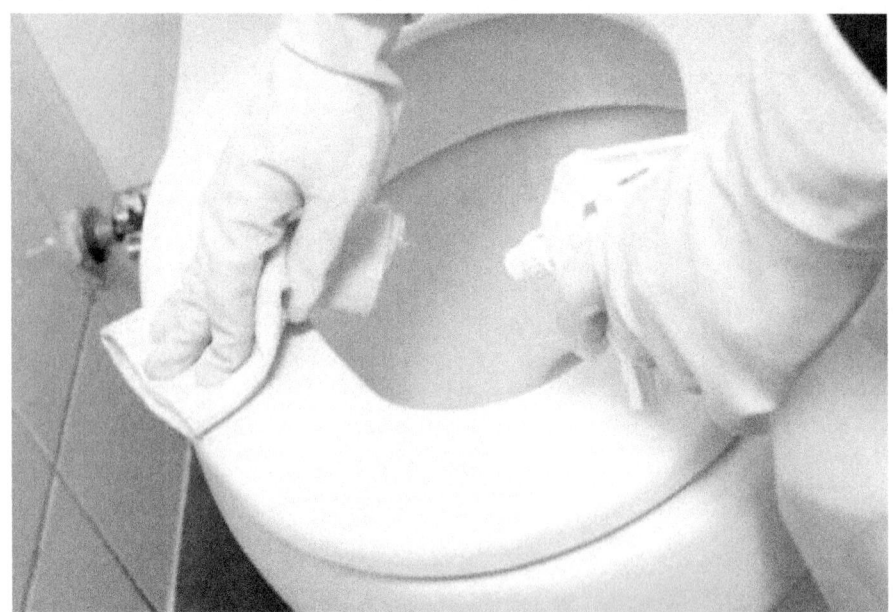

1. Start at the back of the commode. The tank. Wipe down the top and the sides.
2. Unlike the sink and tub you might want to dry each section before you move on to the next.
3. Wipe down the lid and dry it.
4. Wash the seat and dry it.
5. Get in between the tank and the lid and seat and wash right in between there and dry it.
6. Flip the lid and seat up and wipe on the sides on top of the commode and dry them.
7. Then wipe down the rim just inside and dry it.
8. You'll want to flip your wet and possibly your dry rags so you'll be working with clean sides of the rag.
9. Get down on your knees and wash the outside of the commode. Make sure you get everything and dry it.
10. Throw your rags into the wash.

11. Take a toilet brush and scrub the bowl until the yellow stain is gone.
12. If there is still a yellow ring around the bowl, get a pumice stone and rub it against the ring until its gone, or get a strong acid cleaner and scrub it again, it will come off pretty easily.
13. Get some new gloves, or wash the ones you have on.

Rugs

One doesn't really think about rugs in the bathroom, but there they are, and they do make a difference.

1. Take them out of the house and shake them.
2. If they need a deeper cleaning than that check their labels to see if they can be put in the wash.
3. If they can't, follow the directions on the care label to wash them.
4. If they can, throw them in the wash.
5. Don't dry them in the dryer. It could melt the rubber on them and leave a nice big mess for you in the dryer. Throw them on the stairway banister and let them air dry.

Toilet Brush and Cup

Some people use garbage cans for their toilet brush containers, but if you want things to look really nice, containers meant for the toilet brushes work out great.

1. I always figured that when you used the toilet brush and rinsed it out it was pretty ok.
2. But others who think differently say to pour baking soda, hydrogen peroxide and vinegar in the commode and let the brush soak for a while.
3. Flush the commode and rinse the brush off with fresh water.
4. Let it dry by laying it on the toilet seat so that the brush is over the water and close the lid to hold it in place.

5. Now for the container. Whether it be a container especially for the brush, a garbage, or a cup, they will need to be cleaned at least once a month. First, dump out the water that has probably accumulated over the months.
6. Then fill it with hot water and dish soap and scrub it out.
7. Wash the outside too, if it sits next to the commode.
8. Dump out the water and dry it.

Floors

The techniques for the floors vary, depending on whether you have wood, carpet, or tile floors.

1. If you don't want to haul the vacuum to the bathroom you can just take a broom to the floors. Though when deep cleaning it is best to vacuum.
2. If you use a broom, start around the corners and move all the dirt and dust bunnies to the middle of the floor and sweep it into a dust pan and throw it away.
3. If you use the vacuum, get out the hose vacuum and vacuum in the corners and all the difficult places first
4. Then use the regular floor vacuum for the rest of the floor.
5. Get a bucket of water and dish soap and a mop, or a Swiffer and mop the floor.
6. After the floor dries bring in all the stuff you took out.

7. Now if your floors are carpet; my whole hearted advice would be to pull it out and put in something else. It's disgusting!
8. If you really don't care and want to take care of it anyway, get some disinfectant soap and start scrubbing.
9. After everything is scrubbed and you feel as though you've rid the carpet of all bacteria, then either vacuum up all the moisture you can with a wet-dry vacuum.
10. Or get a bunch of towels, lay them all out over the carpet and walk over them until they're soaked; then go and get some more until you're too tired or the towels just won't soak up anymore. You just need to get as much moisture out as possible.
11. Wood floors can be handled the same as tiled floors; just a little bit more carefully.
12. Unless you like to make sure your wood floor is in perfect shape, then use a cleaner meant for wood floors and follow the directions on it.

Garbage's

These aren't too hard to do; they basically just need to be wiped down.

1. Empty the garbage.
2. If it needs to be washed on the inside fill it with water and dish soap and scrub it out.
3. Dump out the water and dry it.
4. If it has a lid just wipe it off and make it clean.
5. Put a new bag in.
6. Bring everything back in.

Time

That was a deep clean procedure. Yet it doesn't take that long to do, especially if you've kept it up throughout the week.

- Getting the cleaners in the sink, tub and commode should take less than a minute.
- The cabinet will probably take half an hour.
- Dusting should take less than five minutes.
- The mirror should take one minute.
- The soap dish one minute.
- The sink about three minutes.
- The tub/showers fifteen minutes.
- Shower curtain would take the longest just because it would go in the wash and the sliding doors should take five minutes
- The bidet probably one minute.
- Commode about three minutes.
- Toilet brush and container five minutes.
- Rugs two minutes.
- Floors five minutes.
- Garbage's five minutes.

So cleaning the bathroom all and all should take about an hour and a half to deep clean, give or take a few minutes. A little less if you've kept up on the bathroom.

Monthly Routine

Now here is the monthly routine. Which you can do while doing your weekly cleaning and just add your monthly routine to it once a month.

- Start with putting your cleaners into the sink, tub/shower, commode and bidet.
- The cabinet can just be checked to see if it needs help at all. If it does, take care of it.
- Dusting the base boards might be a good idea to do once a month.
- The mirror can just be washed the same way as before. Adjusting the mirror once a month will help keep things looking nice and keep the bugs down to a minimal.
- The soap dish can be done the same.
- The sink can be done the same.
- Cleaning the tub/shower doesn't have to be as elaborate as the deep cleaning routine, but time spent cutting down the hard water would be great to do once a month.
- The shower curtain can be left alone. But the shower door tracks if you have them should be done.
- The bidet can be done the same.
- The commode can be done the same.
- The rugs can just be shook.
- Floors can just be swept, and if you think it needs it but don't want to get out the mop and go through the whole procedure of getting a bucket of water and mixing the soap, get a wet rag and wipe down the floors quickly.
- Garbage's can just be wiped down and taken out if necessary.

This monthly routine would probably take an hour.

Weekly Routine

The weekly routine isn't as bad as it sounds. It's definitely not as bad as deep cleaning and it all depends on you; how much trouble you want to go through.

- Obviously put the cleaners in everything that needs to soak.
- You can just wipe down the outside of the cabinet.
- The soap dish can be done the same.
- As can the sink.
- The tub/shower can be done just about the same but you can leave everything in there if you want.
- The shower curtain can be left alone. As can the shower door tracks.
- The bidet if not used a whole lot can get by with just being dusted and wiped out.
- The commode can be done the same.
- The rugs can just be shook.
- The floors can just be swept and left just as it is.
- Garbage's can just be taken out if needed.

If you're pretty fast at this you'll only take thirty minutes tops. If you're still a little bit slow it'll take about forty-five minutes, even less if you've kept up all week.

Daily Routine

Now I keep saying if you keep it up all week. If you're like me and just want to get it done and not worry about it the rest of the week, that's fine, this routine will last all week until you get to it the next week. But here are some little things that you can do throughout the week that would make it a little easier on you the next week when you have to really clean it again.

This is the daily routine or just things to look out for throughout the week to help make the weekly cleaning easier.

- Wipe down the mirror when the specks get a little too noticeable.
- Dry off the faucet and fixtures after you wash your hands.
- Squeegee or dry off the walls after you take a shower or bath.
- Rinse the bidet after you use it.
- Shake the rug out the window when it starts to look dirty.
- If you notice something that just sticks out like a sore thumb, it probably wouldn't take more than a couple minutes to take care of so just do it!

I should say that if you just did the mirror and shook the rugs, everything just looks so much neater, as if you had done everything.

Types of Bathroom Ware

Now I've had my bathrooms in mind this entire time which are ceramic. Here's what to do with other kinds of sinks, tubs and commodes.

- Fiberglass.

Fiberglass is actually not that different from porcelain, it just needs a little more care.

1. So where you would take a chance with an abrasive cleaner on porcelain, you wouldn't even dare with fiberglass.
2. Don't use scouring pads. That just scratches up the surface and makes it harder to clean.
3. You could wax the tub as soon as you get it, or just clean it really good and then wax it. Keep it waxed to ease cleaning.
4. If you can find the manufacturer's instructions to clean the tub, then follow those.

- Stainless steel.

I know it is very unlikely for stainless steel to be in a bathroom, but some people might very well have them, so here goes.

1. Don't use abrasive cleaners.
2. As an inexpensive cleaner, you can just wash the sink or basin with dishwashing detergent and rinse.
3. To avoid water marks you'll want to dry it afterwards.
4. Special stainless steel cleaners also work well.
5. Rubbing alcohol cleans, removes streaks, shines and is safe for the metal.
6. Mineral oil removes streaks and water spots and shines. Use sparingly.
7. Don't use steel wool of soaped steel-wool pads because they will leave rust stains.

8. On that note, it is probably best to not leave anything in it. At least not for a very long time.

- Re-enameled.

Re-enameled tubs are even tougher to clean than fiberglass, because the surface is just a thin layer of finish.

1. So if you want it to last for a good long while, treat it with care.
2. As always, don't use abrasive cleaners and scouring pads on it.
3. Cleaning it regularly will help avoid problems like stains and soap scum that will require tough cleaning.
4. If stains do appear, try a good mild cleaner.
5. If that doesn't work, you might want to call the refinishers to make repairs. Or if the tub is just eating up all your money it might be simpler to just put in a new one.

Apparel

Obviously you don't want to get your nice clothes dirty but you don't have to get into your really grubby clothes either if that's a thing for you.

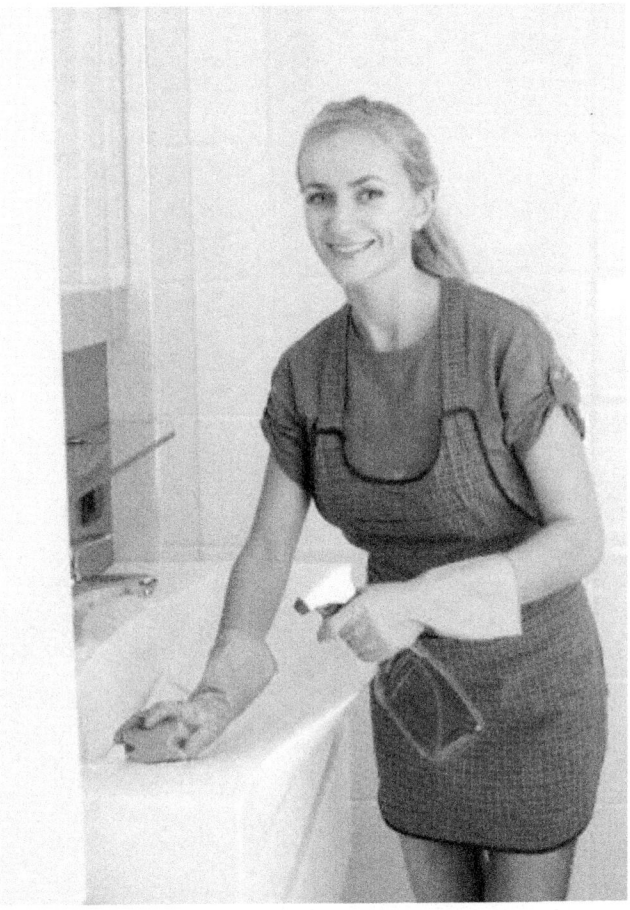

1. Be sure to wear comfortable clothes that allow you to move about freely but aren't too loose.
2. Pull your hair back so that it doesn't get in your way or in something nasty.
3. Wear tennis shoes or shoes with a rubber sole so you don't fall and hurt yourself.

4. Wear disposable rubber gloves, or if you don't have the money to keep buying them, just use the non-disposable ones.
5. Wear a face mask if you are working with strong chemicals or if you just don't like the smell of this job.

Cleaning supplies

Strange as it may seem, you have to be careful with your bathroom ware. Here are some do's and don'ts.

- Do work with non-abrasive cleaners.
- Do work with rags, and in extreme cases a scrubbing pad.
- Don't use scrub pads on everything because after a while they will make the surface dull, and therefor harder to clean.
- Same goes for abrasive cleaners.
- Don't use strong acid cleaners unless it really needs it.
• Now here are some cleaning supplies that I always use. If you have other cleaning supplies you prefer, go ahead and use them.
    - Comet or Ajax
    - The pumice stone
    - Soft scrub pads (if needed)
    - Some old rags

- Baking soda (this works just as well as Comet and is much cheaper)
- Vinegar.
- Clorox, but not very often.

Cleaning on a budget

The way the economy is going right now not many of us have a lot of money to spend on our houses and the expensive cleaning supplies they often need. Here are some cheap ways to clean your bathrooms.

- Baking soda. This by itself works just as well as Comet, though you do have to scrub a little harder.
- White vinegar. This works miracles with hard water and you probably already have it. You just have to let it soak into whatever you're cleaning and it will take it right off.
- Bleach. Bleach is great for making things look fantastic, and disinfecting. But it will not get rid of your soap scum and grime. You have to be careful with bleach too, just because it is so strong. Do not mix it with vinegar. Or with any acid for that matter. It produces a gas that could potentially kill you. If you just love cleaning with bleach, open a window or have the fan going so the fumes can at least be diluted if not carried away by the breeze.
- Rags. Rags are really easy to obtain without ever having to go to the store. Just recycle the old ones that you already have! When the bathroom rags that you use for your face, body and the like, start to look dingy and old, instead of tossing them, just throw them in the cleaning supplies.
- Home-made cleaners. Home-made cleaners are good and cheap to do so long as they don't take up a lot of your time and if the ingredients you need are easy to get, or are already in your house. Otherwise it probably would be cheaper just to get the cleaners you need in the store.

Tips

Here are some tips to help make things easier and keep you sane.

1. Start in the place with the least germs and work your way to the place with the most.
2. Often in hard water areas, hard water will build up to the point where it will clog up your faucets or just look gross. Mix half and half with either white vinegar or lemon juice and water. If you can, unscrew the sink faucet heads and put them in a container of the mixture. Leave them in there until when you take them out you can wipe away the hard water easily. Or you can fill some plastic bags of the mixture and tie them around the faucets and shower heads and let them soak that way.
3. Try not to let clutter accumulate in the bathroom. It just makes it harder to clean when you have to work around stuff that doesn't even belong in there.
4. Get a shower curtain that is machine washable. It will help lighten the load of your mind if not your back when you realize you don't have to break your back trying to wash it. Or whenever it begins to look dingy, just buy a new one. They aren't very expensive at all.
5. If your sinks, tubs and shower drains aren't draining so well, make a wire hook, pull out your drain stopper, stick the hook down into the pipe as far as you can without losing it, and move it around till you feel something. Then pull up. Most likely it will be a most disgusting gob of hair and soap scum. If you don't want to do it, get your husband or another man or the plumbers to do it for you.
6. Vinegar and baking soda work for everything; so do lemons strangely enough.
7. Have the fan going when you take a shower, it will help keep the air dry in the bathroom and help keep away bacteria.

8. Keep an old used toothbrush to use to clean hard to reach corners.
9. If you have more than one bathroom, it is always nice to have the cleaning tools you need in each bathroom so that you don't have to haul everything around with you.
10. If you would rather have all the bathroom cleaning supplies in one place, you can get a container that is small and is easy to carry around.
11. Listen to music when you work. This is probably obvious, but it really helps to make the job seem easier and go faster. Get some upbeat music that you love and will keep you in a good mood throughout the job.

Conclusion

I grew up in a big house with a lot of kids so cleaning the bathrooms was a big job in our family. For some reason we could never keep a cleaning schedule. We would always fall out of practice and have to start up another one at least twice a year. Well one time we stayed on course for a year and I'll tell you why; because we were stuck with one chore for one year each. As luck would have it I was stuck with bathrooms. I was not good at it for a long time, but after a while I could clean it tolerable well, after a lot of trial and error. But as the year went on, I was able to get better and better and faster and faster. I was good at cleaning those bathrooms; if I do say so myself. I even began to think of those bathrooms as if they were mine. Not a great ownership, but I kind of enjoyed it. Even if it is one room that you are in charge of, you at least have the right to tell people how to treat it. So there you have it! I know it seems like a lot just for cleaning a bathroom, but, the longer you clean the bathrooms and the more experience you have, you'll find yourself seeing more and more of what needs to be done without following a list or being told. Not to mention you'll get faster and faster so that even the deep cleaning job won't take so long! I hope you found this book enlightening (if not enjoyable as to what to do with a bathroom and how to care for it. Have fun!

Author Bio

Rachel Redden is a writer who was raised with her large family in the mountains. She has grown up around animals all her life and finds great joy in them. She has been writing since she was twelve and has enjoyed every minute of it. Rachel still lives with her loving family in the mountains of Wyoming.

Our books are available at:

1. Amazon.com
2. Barnes and Noble
3. Itunes
4. Kobo
5. Smashwords
6. Google Play Books

Health Learning Series

How to Clean Toilets

GRANDMA'S
NATURAL REMEDIES
AND ANCIENT HERBAL
BEAUTY RECIPES
Volume 1
HEALTH LEARNING SERIES
DUEEP J SINGH AND J DAVIDSON
GRANDMA'S
NATURAL REMEDIES
AND ANCIENT HERBAL
BEAUTY RECIPES
Volume 2
HEALTH LEARNING SERIES
DUEEP J SINGH AND J DAVIDSON
GRANDMA'S
NATURAL REMEDIES
AND ANCIENT RECIPES
GRANDMA'S CURE FOR OBESITY
GRANDMA'S CURE FOR THE COMMON COLD
Volume 3
HEALTH LEARNING SERIES
DUEEP J SINGH AND J DAVIDSON
GRANDMA'S
NATURAL REMEDIES AND
ANCIENT HERBAL RECIPES
Volume 4
HEALTH LEARNING SERIES
DUEEP J SINGH AND J DAVIDSON
GRANDMA'S
HERBAL LORE
ANCIENT HERBAL RECIPES AND REMEDIES
Volume 5
HEALTH LEARNING SERIES
DUEEP J SINGH AND J DAVIDSON
GRANDMA'S
ANCIENT
BEAUTY REMEDIES
FROM HER KITCHEN
Volume 6
HEALTH LEARNING SERIES
DUEEP J SINGH AND J DAVIDSON
GRANDMA'S
EASY TO USE TIPS
IN THE KITCHEN AND OUTDOORS
Volume 7
HEALTH LEARNING SERIES
DUEEP J SINGH AND J DAVIDSON
GRANDMA'S
HOUSEHOLD HINTS AND RECIPES
USING TIME TESTED
ECONOMICAL TIPS IN YOUR HOME
75 Tips
Remove Stains
Peel Tomatoes
Perfect Pies
HEALTH LEARNING SERIES
DUEEP J SINGH AND J DAVIDSON
GRANDMA'S
NATURAL REMEDIES
AND ANCIENT RECIPES
ALL 5 BOOKS IN 1
HEALTH LEARNING SERIES
DUEEP J SINGH AND J DAVIDSON

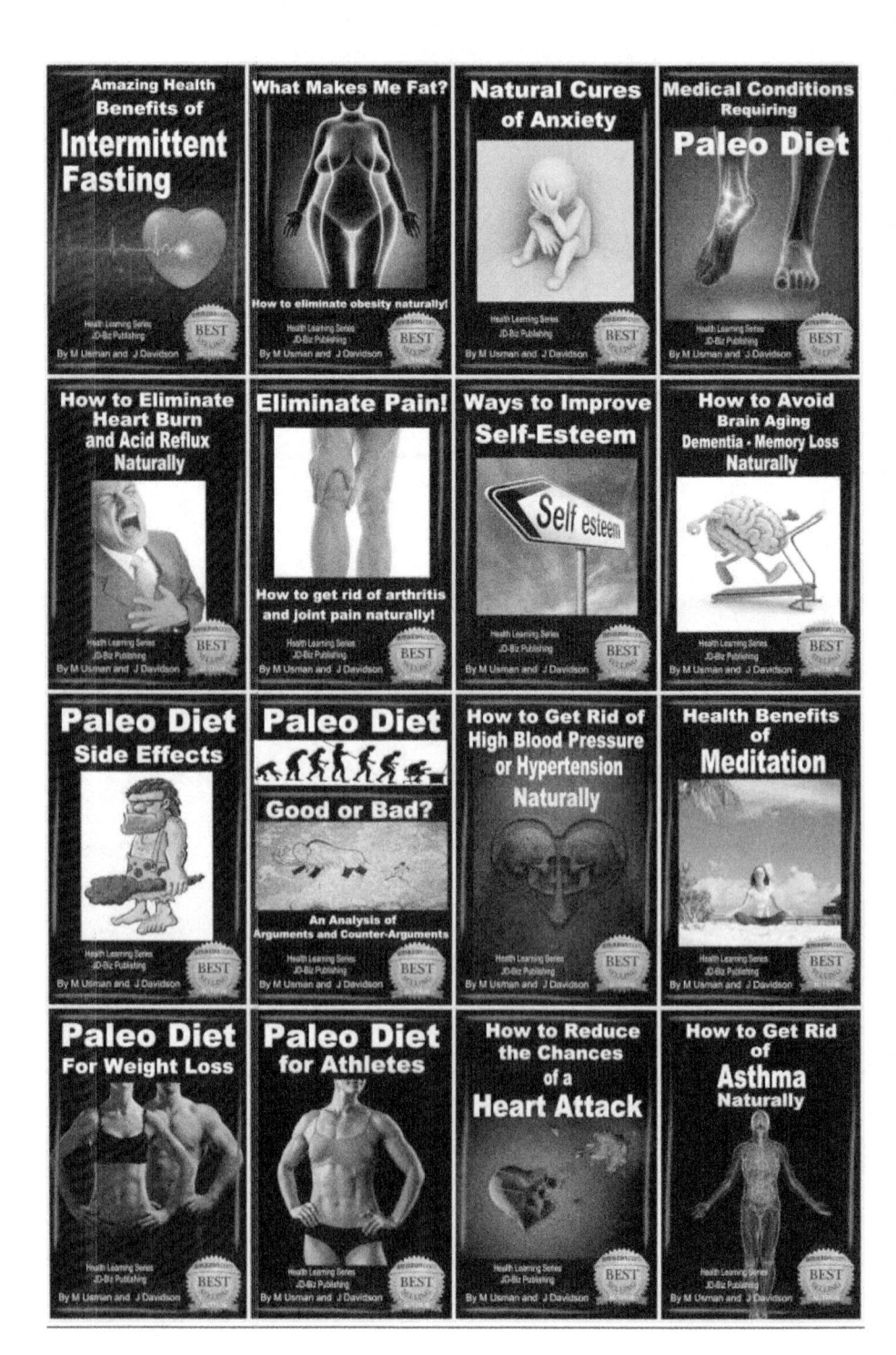

Amazing Animal Book Series

How to Clean Toilets — Page 45

Dog Books for Kids

How to Clean Toilets
Page 46

Learn To Draw Series

How to Build and Plan Books

Entrepreneur Book Series

Publisher

JD-Biz Corp

P O Box 374

Mendon, Utah 84325

http://www.jd-biz.com/

Read more books from

Mendon Cottage Books

P O Box 374, Mendon Utah 84325

Printed in Great Britain
by Amazon